Learning To Breathe Underwater
Jason Elliot

follow me into the dark
i'll show you where it all went wrong
black out the sun and fall asleep
cross my heart and rest in peace

leave me alone

loneliness comes and goes
it's the seed that plants every thorn and destroys every single rose
but like the seasons, it always comes back and the feeling is never the same
patterns repeat but the drops of water differ in every tidal wave
if i let my light burn out and i blow a fuse, i may not have a way to fix it
isolation and acceptance of it are the two things i've become most familiar with
so i'll sit here side by side with the darkness in my head
not thinking about the things i've done, but just the things i regret leaving unsaid
why do my feelings feel like such a sin?
they've become the one thing i'm becoming terrified to befriend and let in
i feel alone and neglected, hollow and rejected
nothing but an empty shell, weak and unprotected
will i ever know the feeling of not feeling alone?
or will i find comfort in the distance and fear the idea of getting close?

the constant

i hit rock bottom but the cement never dried

so i kept on sinking until the pavement started to eat me alive

it's a long way to the top, so i wonder if i should even try

i experienced life so now i can experience what it's like to die

i'm on the other side
and oddly enough it feels more real than life

i'm not just a ghost
i'm an entity and i can still feel my bones

i don't have a heartbeat
just a constant cycle of nightmares and daydreams

hologram

some nights are darker than the rest
sometimes there's nothing but a broken heart struggling to beat
inside my chest
and lately, my dreams don't seem like dreams anymore
just a vivid memory constantly pounding and scratching at my
minds door
it begs to be let out, but it hurts too much and i'm too scared to be
touched
so leave me numb and leave me bruised
when you lose your world, you become one with the broken and
abused

no one will ever see how broken i truly am
it's as if my entire persona is nothing but a hologram
i'm a ghost of myself because i'm ashamed of my weakness

i'll never believe that this is the life that i'm left with

my intentions are like tidal waves
they look strong but end up washing everything away
my dreams are like the city streets
covered in filth and begging for peace

---

i need to figure out which bridges to cross and which ones to burn
i started to notice the difference between learning lessons and
lessons learned
while my intentions are far from sight but close in mind
leave my words where you found them because the truth is better
left behind

i'll be perfect, i promise

people always come and go
but the hardest thing is when you realize that the memories don't
if i wear my heart on my sleeve, you can cut off all my limbs
i'm so sick of letting everything that kills me get inside my skin

embracing my nightmares is easier than letting go of my dreams
i know where each road will take me, it's just a matter of what each
one brings
my biggest fear is holding on and i have a grip on letting go
maybe my weaknesses are the only thing that i'm strong enough to
show

i've become more scared of life then i've ever been of death
just because i can count my scars, doesn't mean i can count my
breath
i never thought my mind could outweigh my heart
because my thoughts never end up the way i intended from the start

i hope you can find me, just like the ripples in the ocean waves
and i'll come as long as i can stay
i can't promise i'll be perfect but i promise i'll be okay

okay someday

heartbreak is haunting and beautiful
how we can feel something so much it almost seems unusual
it's the worst kind of pain that lingers and doesn't go away
but it makes you feel alive
the feeling of dying a thousand times

i know one day i'll be okay again
i'll move on by myself without the help of someone else's hand
just let me catch my breath again
before i lose the grip it's in
i'm not falling for anyone again

i'll leave the light on to make sure of it

out of sorts

if blood is thicker than water
why am i drowning in both?
my knowledge and memories are clashing together
i can't tell what matters the most

if my dreams could step into reality
somehow it's not far off...

everything has become a blur
my tunnel vision is only her
with a one-track mind, i'm falling behind
tying my veins together so i can unwind

don't cry for me when i go away
i said all the things that i had to say
why does it matter if i lose everything?
i've been out of sorts for too long anyway

run wild

there are two worlds inside of me
one of darkness and one i can see
but the one thing i never understood is how they both seem to be the same
how can i be a faded echo and a lantern's flame?
it seems easier said than done once everything is said and done
and now it's too late, but time is still existent and running wild with relevance
so is it ever really too late?

listen to me when i express every single thing that i've ever been afraid of
i've been terrified to live the life i'm cursed with, a blessing of sheer lack of endurance
waking up, conquering sleep, the process it takes to repeat
the struggle exists within me and i'm not the idle hand, i'm the pendulum swing
but my strings are wearing thin

my biggest fear was not facing myself
my biggest fear was losing everything and losing the chance to have anything else

this is for every statement i refused to relate to the state of my conscience
fixated on the realization of the darkness of this realization.
more like an awakening, a rare case of metamorphosis in a newly founded rotation.

i was never bored, just angry
and i was never lost
...just misplaced

bummer

maybe i'm just better off alone
i couldn't wait to be king but now i'm sick of the throne
maybe i should've thrown myself to the wolves when i had the
chance
instead of being prey, i just became one of the rest

left out, dried out, i'm alone now
i still find myself getting lost in my hometown
heartbreak, heartache, it's all the same now
even in the shallow water, i hope i still drown
nothing's perfect, nothing gold can stay
i'll leave the rusting imperfections for another day
flawless flaws now seem to fade with you
please forget me so i can be at peace, too

funeral

my insecurities are like a hearse
i'll carry them to my grave
the only thing that makes it worse
is knowing that they'll never go away

meet me at the lighthouse
even if the lights are out
i just want the scene of the crash to be beautiful
i want you to see that i'm tearing down your pedestal
watch me take my pain away
i'll drink and drive so i can die in flames
i'll make it quick so i don't feel the pain
now i'm gone but i know you're still okay

don't celebrate my life, it wasn't beautiful

i always fantasize about what it'll be like at my funeral

happiness is always the hardest thing to find
it seems to be the first thing you lose and the last thing you leave
behind

---

when the winds change, i start to walk along a faded line
stuck in a rut but that's the only time when i feel like i'm chasing a
high
i try not to turn my disease into a habit
addicted to the attention, i'll admit that i'm an addict
i don't know where these feelings came from
reassure me that i'm not doing this all wrong
keep my negativity in the spotlight
i lost myself completely before i turned 29

---

i can be the echo through the mountains
and the comfort of your dreams
the youth inside your fountain
and the stitches to your seam

drift

it was never my choice to live my life this way
feeling a constant burden at the times when i'm awake
lay me down and let me fall asleep
i can't feel death if it's only in my dreams

let me swallow these bitter pills
so i can drift away against my will
so i can be numb enough to feel the cure
i'll fall asleep and i'll fall even more

i'm stressed out and i feel alone
i'm by myself but i feel at home
it's like a crowded room inside my head
a sea of strangers that i've never met

and if i say i need to let go
the last word i want to hear is, "no"
please don't let me sink, i've already gone too low
i can't say that i'm sorry because that's something that i'll never know
i'm not selfish, i'm just selfless
i'm lost in myself and that's what i live with

the other side

trembling in my footsteps
and fighting with my own mind
all the terrible things that i've done, they've come out from the places they hide
and every unspoken word is something i keep to myself
somehow i'll have to explain this all so i don't wind up in hell
no, i can't make this right again
all i can do is become a different man
i shouldn't be scared of myself, but i'll admit, i'm terrified
i wish i could tell the truth but i feel safer behind these lies

there's a difference between being alone and feeling alone
when the doors are open, the world is your home
but i've been hurting too much from hurting too much
i'm not holding back tears, i'm just not saying enough

so save me, save me once again
and stay with me 'til the end
time isn't on my side
it's waiting on the other end
it's waiting for me to die
i'm just washed up, like a message in a bottle that was thrown out to sea
i'm a sinner, not a man, and that's all i'll ever be

if there's a place between hell and my heart

please help me find what it is that's tearing me apart

deep rest

it's not what you're searching for
it's what you find in the end that counts the most
and although it seems that i'm living, i can't help but to feel like a ghost

have you ever had trouble recognizing your own reflection?
as if what's staring back at you is only a misconception
every mistake i've made, has only been building me a personal hell
and it hurts to know that i hate myself for knowing myself so well

you see, my thoughts aren't like yours, and my dreams are far from ordinary
if you could see inside my mind, you would see these things are involuntary
i never listen to my heart, i always listen to the world around me
but that's never worked, i need some sort of change of priority

so, i've learned to turn my intentions into questions
where will i be after this is said and done and after i'm released from this depression?
will someone be there to care for me and to lift me off my feet?
or will i end up back where i was, with nowhere to go, completely broken and beat

i have the ambition to let myself go
but i lack the guts to push myself and open the wounds that i've sewn

i've always hated the fact that i can't see myself from the outside in
my patience with everything is forever running thin
there's a part of me that no one knows and a part of me that i let

show
but the one thing that's inside of me, i'm too ashamed for the world to see
inside i am fragile, broken apart, scared and alone
this head on my shoulders i'm afraid to call home

i hate these demons that crawl around and ruin my dreams
they take what i want and turn them into things that i need
if i keep pulling myself through this, it's only gonna push the world away
nothing is worth letting go of if it's always gonna stay

there is no escape, for now, i'll create my own atmosphere
where i can float off to someplace else, somewhere far away from here
and in the end, i'll never get over my fear of getting old
and in the end, we all have to die, or so i've been told

i'm not okay with accepting death, but what more can i do?

maybe i'll find peace the day my body is taken from this room

bloom

most of the time, i feel invisible to everyone and everything around
me
and it hurts that no one understands and plays blind to things i know
that they can clearly see
it's like walking through a field where the flowers are too afraid to
bloom
because any sight of beauty in life is too much for a wasted soul and
tortured youth
and if i have nothing at all, i have nothing to lose

though all this time, i've been told to keep quiet while i had
something more to prove

little hell

maybe a little hell is all i need
maybe heaven forgot about me
but maybe that's okay
death called me and it's on the way

bring me back to the place that i call home
tell me something even if it's something that i already know
i need to know...will i die here?
will i ever let go of this?
i need to know...will i die here?
a little hell is worth more than bliss

read me all the fairy tales
the fiction that could never fail
to lift up all my spirits
the ones i have to live with
put a little faith in my insecurity
a little hell will bring out the best of me

there's too much water in my lungs
but i'm not drowning
there's too much fire in my heart
but i'm still not burning
and there's too much going through my mind
it keeps playing backwards, living constantly in a state of rewind

if you see my demons, don't let them run
i need to bring them back to where they came from

i am a little hell, isn't that all we need?
you can put out the flames but i'm still human and i still bleed

i am a little hell, can you find out where it all went wrong?
i asked the devil on my shoulder and he said it's been this way all
along

my isolation

we are all we know
i am nothing but lost hope
maybe one day things will change
but i'm used to things being this way
you can fall out of line so many times
until the last one breaks your mind

i can't calm down, and i won't come down
from this place that wore me out
i'm too far gone, and i've made it clear
the only thing i need right now is for you to leave me here

stop saying i'm not better off this way
just because i'm hurt doesn't mean i'm not okay
i found peace in broken pieces
i found love within my demons
i found that if you tell yourself a thousand lies
it feels like you're living a thousand different lives
and i'd rather be consumed by my own isolation
than wake up to a world that i pretend to be in

poison me

you can't start a fire without the flame
repeat the patterns, don't be scared to look away
we need to leave some things behind
leave them to sit in the passing of time
how can you dig a grave if you don't know how deep to go?
how can you measure how much of the earth is worth my soul?

poison me
i promise that i'll be alright
i'd rather lose it all than face this fight
regret is something real
it's more than what i feel
so poison me
so i forget it all
don't help me when i start to fall

let's watch the seasons change
maybe i can start to admire the rain
bringing back the peace i thought i lost
a never-ending cycle of never learning the cost
of what it means to come full circle
after all, every trial is just a rehearsal

learn from your mistakes
don't follow the tracks that i have made
i will never listen to myself
where was god when i cried for help

there's a pattern when you're nowhere to be found
it's like i'm going crazy
finding balance between silence and the sound

take your time when you poison me

blistered

some days i feel nothing
yet that seems to hurt the most
i'm not broken, i'm just empty
i don't feel like the real me
i lost all of my luck
and never had a chance to give anything a chance
it's like the world sees me walking forward
and suddenly a wall is built
so i turn the other way
and it all just turns to black

i'm just a raindrop lost at sea
you will never find me and that's okay
i tell myself i forgot what it's like to love
but then i wonder if i ever really loved at all
i just feel alone, i guess
even if all eyes are on me
in the end, i'm still in my head
wondering what the world would be like without me

would you forget my name?
or how long would it take until you do?
would you judge me for how i felt?
i'm so scared of being myself more than anything,
even when i'm not around you
treat me like you would a passing storm
wait for me to leave and then admire the aftermath

this is not a cry for attention
just a simple moment of truth
while i can admit life itself could be worse
it certainly isn't good

and i can't bring myself to find a reason to think otherwise

can you change my mind?
can you open up my blistered eyes?
tell me all the things i need to hear
all the things i've never heard
no wonder why i'm so down on myself
i'm my own worst critic and the only one watching...

i fell out of love, if that's what it was
because i was scared to be in it
i was scared of getting hurt
i still am
everyone is out to get me
and if they're not

change my mind

it's a shame that you all share the same heart
searching for the next person that you can slowly rip apart
just like a house of mirrors, you're one of many, but you're all the
same
the worst thing i ever did was let my heart beat to the pattern of your
name

---

i wish that i could get inside your head
and hear all those things you said were better left unsaid
but the lines we drew are starting to fade
and like a leaf in the wind, being lost and then found, it all seems the
same
so if i play the ocean and you play the waves
just promise me that we won't lose track of our pace

---

i could've sworn that we were soul mates
but now you're just everything that my soul hates

what i have to live with

i'd rather lose my dignity than drag it through hell just to end up
alone and scared
even if i'm nowhere to be found, at least that's still somewhere
i might be nobody but i'm not invisible
i might be somebody but i'm not invincible
and if someone cares, shine some light on my soul
but i'd rather be in the dark, where i feel most at home

if i wear my heart on sleeve, tear me apart limb from limb
one thing i've always wanted is to feel numb while learning how to
live
my sanity eats my pain away, and sometimes the other way around
there's a difference between being found in the noise and getting lost
in the sound

help me pick up the pieces
i'm the puzzle that was incomplete to begin with
i never knew myself, and thats always been my weakness
and that's all i know about myself, that's what i have to live with

dying on demand

i'm so sick of being lost in my own mind
i'm not afraid of the dark, i just hate knowing that i may never find the light
i hate the person that inhabits this vessel of bone, muscle and skin
i don't know right from wrong and i'm way too broken to find a place to fit in

have you ever lived inside a dream?
not the one that captures you when you fall asleep
it's something that you can't physically see but it pulls you away from reality
because sometimes i pretend that i'm not real, like it's a privilege to learn to feel
and something deep down inside of me knows this is not someone that i want to be
i need to snap out of this miserable fantasy and just run with the wind until it catches up with me

place my body beneath the floor
i don't need to be here but i still need more
i need the answers to what happens when i leave
so let me eavesdrop on everything i'll miss from right beneath your feet
i'm sorry for hurting you, i'm sorry for hurting myself
i'm sorry for hurting the both of us and putting us through a certain kind of hell
i took on this ghostly void and i robbed you of your mental stability and what was left of your joy
so maybe i'm the demon, the one that you always feared
i know you can see right through me now but i remember the days when you'd apologize for demanding me to disappear

i'm sick of crying out for help and trying to escape through permanently locked doors

i hate knowing that the little bit of hope i had bled out and now has sunken into the hardwood floor

i cut out my happiness with the sharpest blade i could find and then i gouged my eyes out with the idea that maybe someday things will be fine

maybe i'm meant to be like this...broke, useless and the last one to ever be missed

always left out and socially dead, always regretting every single word i've said

i hate myself and that'll never change

i hate myself and i'm always the one taking the blame

struggle

i have this overwhelming fear of death
i count my days and i count every single breath
it's something that consumes me and keeps me from functioning
normally
i just wish my instincts would teach me the rules of acting morally
it's my lack of sleep and my fear to dream
that leads me to believe that everything's the opposite of what it
seems
because every time i close my eyes, i drift off into another place
another world where i have some sort of faith
and even if i believe in something, how will i know that nothing is
pretend
so i'll be here wondering when it'll happen, and how it will end
who will care and who will cry
these are the things that eat me up alive inside
and i'm telling you this is no way to live
thinking about what happens after is something that i'll never come
to terms with
it's the hardest thing that i'll ever have to face
death, when you come for me, please make it quick and take me to a
better place
and if it's not these thoughts that keep me up at night
it's my fear of life itself that leaves me paralyzed
but what scares me the most, is i know that i've sinned
my mindless decisions led me to this place that i'm in
and if there's a god, i just hope that he sees
i only wanted good for this world, i just struggled to believe

turn off the lights

and so they say, let it rain on your parade
but does it make a difference if the weather never changed?
i'm not the sticks and i'm not the stones but i hold the heart that's
behind these bones
so while you create something out of nothing only to destroy me
remember you're the one that kept my roots from growing

i've been let down and i've been the let down
and i've been the right one in and the one left out
i've seen both sides of the story, and i've walked a mile in a
stranger's shoes
i learned how to live my life without being as heartless as you

but can you say this is easy?
it's so short lived but is it right to let it swing by so freely?
be the catcher to my pitcher, it's never one strike and then you're out
we need to breathe, settle in and figure out what it's really about
it takes two to tango and one to lead, two to love and one to leave,
one to fly and one to teach
but it always takes two to learn what we both need

and it never occurred to me
how one can leave someone in the dark so easily
when you find the light, you create a fire, let it burn and watch it
expire
but i never understood much about anything, and maybe that's my
fault
how you can lead somebody to believe that they meant anything at
all?

i'm not hurt, because i've always been this way
disappointed seems like the wrong word to say
but i'll admit i'm misled and maybe i'm naive

will i ever learn to stop wearing my heart on my sleeve?

fake in love

have you ever watched as your world fell apart
it's hard to tell where mountains end if you're standing far enough
but i've seen forest fires shine like the sun
and i've seen glaciers melt and come undone
i've seen nature die and i'm aging quick
i need to find some time to feel something more than this

i guess that i've been fake in love
i guess that i was never enough
i guess that i've been fake in love and out of line
i guess i forgot how to find myself after being lost for all this time
fake in love and second best
i need some time for myself to relax and reset

no one

i can't remember the last time i was satisfied with everything in life
i have the hope to stand on but there are too many steps to climb
for once, i miss the feeling of being happy with myself
sometimes i just accept that nothing is the only something i've ever
felt

i don't need change as much as change needs me
there's something inside of me that tells me i don't have to be weak
it's just, when you're so used to carrying the world on your shoulders
you can't help but fear you've gone nowhere the more you grow
older

i've been slowed down in my tracks because i refused to learn how
to run
and i've kept my past with me because looking ahead is no different
than staring into the sun
the more the glare leaves you blind
you can't help but refuse to let go of what you should've left behind

but in the end, i only have myself to blame for this
i raised myself on the bliss of ignorance
and i may have drowned in every ocean and revived myself in every
sea
but the only thing i didn't do, is let my absence of purpose get the
best of me

i've worn a mask and i've said things that i never meant to say
don't ever trust a man that can't keep up with his own games that he
plays
my absence of purpose is my absence of life
i've always doubted myself with every tear that i've cried

i don't hate myself, i hate what i let myself become
there's a difference between where i'm going to and where i started
from

i've only begun my battle because i'm too scared to start a war
i'll break both of my knees before i try to find something that i
should stand for
maybe my trust in anyone is something that's too much to bear
so tie me to the tracks so i can spill my guts from here to there

you see, i'm ready and i'm willing to kill myself
but i don't have the courage to accept my fate in hell
when the worst of me has taken over the best of me
i am no one, and i have set myself free

if i can't find peace within myself, how will i find it in anyone else?

relocate

i can't help but to seem lost
not so much out of place, just as if i slipped away from something
familiar
maybe it's the way i taught myself to sleep
i convinced myself it was a lot like living
except the bad dreams wouldn't seem so real
lucid dreaming only means living unconsciously
and i've found the monsters hiding under my bed
they crawled into my mind and have become part of me
maybe i'm not lost, maybe i'm just hiding
relocate me

resurface

lead me to my shadow, it's the only thing that lets me know i'm alive
buried and broken
torn apart and spit out
i may have spent my life beneath everyone around me
but i am free to live by my own will
changes become me
a stranger now to deceit
i am reborn, i have resurfaced

rediscover

following the footsteps of a tortured past will only rip open your
scars
if death doesn't heal your wounds, then forgetfulness may help guide
your way
amnesia is something i've always wanted but couldn't quite hold
onto
i've loved once, but I'm not sure why
have i found the golden truth?
the seeker becomes the thief
desperate for self-moderation
i've become a traveler of hope and a myth of familiar faith
take me to where i came from, this place i once called home
spineless no more, i am whole

the power of entity, my rediscovery

some sort of meaning

there's nothing worse than the constant need to constantly try to feel alive
i know the world will never be good enough
so i should learn not to ever set my standards so high
i never knew that the one thing i wanted would be the one thing i was
always afraid to find
life: if i could hold the word as an entity as something i could feel
maybe i wouldn't be so afraid to actually act upon it in a recurring existence
that i'll always be too fragile to accept
i am my own nightmares...
i always pretend like it's my mind playing tricks on me...
but in the end, i'm the joker and i'm the thief
playing games and then stealing them away just to leave me in a state of
confusion again and again...
"let me listen to the sound of my own voice," i said to myself, convincing
myself i'm capable of some sort of change
the only change i'll ever be capable of is the capability of not changing
just like i pretend to sleep underwater so i can force myself to stop breathing
it's not suicide if in your mind, you're still alive
it's times like these that make me thankful for the pressure of the tidal waves
because without them, i wouldn't feel anything at all
maybe dying isn't my best option, but living as second best and never first
priority to anyone doesn't seem much better
black sheep is something i would call myself
like an angel without wings, a diva that cannot sing, another bone to break
in a body that's only become empty
i need to hold some sort of meaning because the only thing i ever seem to
stand for is the wishful thinking that one day that'll play out differently
even if i were a trophy, at least i would make you proud for a short period
of time...
before something better comes along and i end up just collecting dust
just like memories hold true love and fade away into something in between
that and lust
but i won't and i can't sit here and pretend that i'm fine and that everything
is okay
because i've lost my mind so long ago
that i can't even save myself from me

move forward, step back, lose yourself, repeat
replay the nightmares that disguise themselves as daydreams
if playing dead means falling asleep
prescribe me the medicine that'll keep me at ease

in formation

i don't regret anything but i know i've made mistakes
but i take ease in these mistakes because that means i've learned
and that also means i've tried to breach my comfort
but sometimes my comfort becomes an unsettling entity that i force
myself into living with
and no, i'm not running away from my problems, i never would
but when it comes down to it…
i've become paralyzed in a state of mind
and this state of mine has only led me to lead myself into a
conscience of guilty conscience
my imperfections don't make me, but they shape me
my scars don't kill me, but they destroy me
and my words don't break me, but they hurt everyone else around
me
and my actions? well, they don't define me, but they're what
paralyzes me

change me and recreate me so i can accept my acceptance of
imperfection
i'd rather let the world know of all my flaws rather than to keep
hiding behind them
i could keep my true self hidden like the dark side of the moon
but the me that i choose to let you see is a lunar masterpiece
constantly changing like the seasons
except i don't rain and i don't snow,
i just brush it off and pretend like i don't know…
like i don't know how real the pain is…
or how the mistakes i've made is the hell i now believe in
a smile and a word can only cover so much
before life, love, and every emotion you can't possibly escape from
washes it all away

this is not a cry out for remorse,
it's a final testimony that i need to scream before i go completely
hoarse
and if it's not the ghost of me that i forced into this untimely course
you'll be sure to find me hidden behind the doors,
under the floorboards searching for something more to permanently
keep at ease and in store

leave me here to remember me
i hope that i find solitude in the desolation of sleep
i won't forget what i've done, but i'll forgive what i've been through
my history is not just history, just like history has never been that to
begin with
my story, your story and ours are just the testing of time,
an uncertain chain of events that leads one circumstance into another
and when all is said and done, you win or you lose
we can't all be winners, but we can all be pawns
and just to be a part of the game is what makes it beautiful
run away, not from yourself, but from reality
honor your placement, darling
we are all man-made, fragile and far from invincible
but that doesn't mean we need to feel any of those things, that doesn't
mean we can't be anything and everything that we've always longed
to be

a thousand voices

i shouldn't have to choose if i should sink or swim
you don't know who i am or where i've been
i'm not the one under the spotlight but i'm not afraid to shine in the
dark
if i've learned anything, it's not to become the devil you avoided
from the start

i am a prophet fallen from grace
what once stood tall now lost it's place

in patterns of dust, i've followed a trail composed of empty promises
and regret
becoming a mockery among the ones you love
and the ones you thought would forget

remember everything as if it were paved in gold
we are but only memories and stories told

when this world learns to comprehend intentions from misguided
choices
i will be the one to lead a march of a thousand voices

some things are better left unsaid
i paid my dues, i know what lies ahead
some things are better off this way
i never meant for this to become torn and frayed

pain is too real to let slip away, i've found the hope to remind me i'm
okay

we all make mistakes and become the burdens we hate

but it's never too late to stand up for the reasons of the chances we take
collecting my words and assorting every move that i'll make

i never thought living would kill every breath that i take

glisten

i used to be happier when i was with you
and i wish that you felt the same way too
you're the sun that makes the sunrise shine
and the stars that surround the moon to make it glisten every night
i wish we could take back every bad memory and every single fight
so we can rewind to a time when we knew that it was love at very
first sight

i miss the way that we spoke, the way that we slept
there are too many things i would never forget
the way you looked at me, and i knew i was loved
but a broken heart can never heal
if you can't figure out what the stitches are made of

it was the hopeless dreams and the endless nights
where forever wasn't in the distance, it was where we stood in time
you made my world stand still, and nothing else mattered
i wish i knew what went wrong, instead of replaying it over in
patterns

time has passed, and so have we
maybe we haven't noticed, but we're nothing but a memory
you need to be loved, you deserve it, it's true
and if i have to wait forever, then that's what i'll do

i'd rather wait than ever risk a chance of losing you

ripped silver lining

sometimes hope seems more like hell
and that's the hardest truth that there is to tell
and i don't fear loneliness, but loneliness...it fears me
that's why it grows so attached, because it's too afraid to leave

sometimes when you hit rock bottom
you keep on falling further and further
because when denial leaves you blind, you're forced to become the
observer
it's the struggle to see past the pain
to wonder if things will be okay
but, i can promise you there isn't always a silver lining
just a constant search for something you'll forget you were finding

all i've learned so far—
is that you can't open a wound without having one from the start
my stitches ripped open the minute i let you into my heart
and i all i ever wanted was to love and be loved
but now the thought of it is what i've become most afraid of

i've used denial as an excuse, just like the drugs that i seek to use
i've mixed up attention for abuse, because i like them both the same
because i like the bitter pain
of that little bit of an escape, the one that takes me far away
i can't get too close to you, i can't see what you see through
my transparent heart, my lucid dreams
my broken soul, tangled and torn at the seams
I've never wished for death before
but my life has no potential of becoming anything more
so, leave me here, to understand love as fear
and watch me turn into nothingness, will it matter if i disappear?

it's so hard to cope with something you don't know how to deal
with
lighting the fuse at both ends and making the best of it
i'm lost in myself, but i guess that's another story to tell
i found myself in nothingness, it's what i relate to the most
the space between the living and me is bonded by a ghost

---

i hope that i die in my sleep
so i won't have to feel a thing
i hope that i die in my dreams
so it's almost the real thing

i'm fine

i've been better but i've been worse
i guess once you stop believing in blessings, you could live through
a curse
because without negative emotion, we're nothing but blank space in
motion
nowhere to go but always somewhere to hide
as you get older it becomes easier to watch your nightmares come
alive
and to watch your dreams die
and, no, i'm not saying i got this whole thing twisted
all i'm saying is that whoever created this world has me painted the
victim
with everyone i love and meet, and every single stranger on the
street
are consistently conducting a symphony of fingers pointed directly
at me
like i'm the one who's blind, like i'm the one who's left behind
like i'm the one who doesn't deserve life…
but only deserves to die
i'm sick of never being right
i'm sick of never being able to find the darkness when i grow tired
of the light
because sometimes it hurts
sometimes it hurts so much that i don't even bleed anymore, i just
become numb to it
i lose all feeling and losing it all is the only savior i ever met
because taking false promises—and false hopes—and hanging them
up with all of my belongings on the wall of my own decency and
kindness
has only been a constant spiral downfall
making me dizzy before i crash, making the momentum of the fall

eternally last

so i'll lash out and run away from everyone and everything,
wondering over and over again why these things keep happening
breaking my bones along the way because i feel more alive when
i'm far from okay

fighting and screaming in my sleep because it's easier to keep silent,
at least if that's what you believe

and i'm not meant to be the one who's cold…

or the one who's cast to stone

by a simple word or a simple unknown

i force myself into this pain by forcing myself to expose my shame
to ones i love the most, ironically, the ones that have also hurt me
once they got too close

but i am not anyone's shining armor, i'd be a fool to believe anyone
who says they'll stick around for a little longer

maybe i'm not meant to be remembered, just a memory to
eventually become dismembered

toss me into the sea, where this whole time i believe i was meant to
be

to be cradled and destroyed throughout the waves, helpless and
alone without the will to be saved

keep an eye out for my ghost, i'm sure i'll pass through from time to
time

and if i leave this world with anything, just remember you should've
never believed me when i said everything with time will be just fine

monster in me

i hate myself too much to be by myself
i hate my mind too much, it's an inevitable personal hell
i need to grow with someone because i'm too weak to do it on my
own
my heart doesn't beat correctly or on time unless it's owned
some people like silence but i need the noise
some people like the solitude but i can't stand the sound of my own
voice
maybe someday someone will be my saving grace
until then, i'll struggle to stay lost pacing around in the same place

if i were to be honest, i'm feeling more than hopeless
if i were to be open, i've kept my thoughts unspoken
i thought that in my head, they would be safe
turns out this whole time they only needed an escape
i'm too down on myself to fall anymore
the last bridge i burned was the one that started this war
don't take a match to your mind when your heart is drenched in
kerosene
because when you end up in flames, you bring out the monster...
the monster that's me

only another

if love has taught me anything
it's to watch your step before you fall into it
and if i could take back everything
i wouldn't, but be careful for what you wish

i hate to say that where we ended up is such a shame
i just never expected someone like you to change
they say you never know what you have until it's gone
and i could wait for you to come back but that would mean i'm just
waiting to be wrong

i felt at home with you, and now i have a cold world to look forward
to
where is the comfort that we found in each other?
instead of being the one, you're only another
just add it to list, of the chances that i missed

to find what i needed the most, the very idea of happiness

far from perfect

please, just grant me one last wish
make it easy to just exist
i know i have to stay just one more day
but if i had the choice, i would throw it all away

i will never understand happiness or the pursuit of it
and i will never come to grips with how hard growing up hits
so maybe if i took the time to analyze just where i am, and my place
in life
i'd see a world with brand new eyes
but in my mind, i'm forcefully blind
yet in my heart, this hurt is only a disguise

things don't get better, but they eventually change
some things you don't get over, but you get through the pain
and when your world feels like it's over, sometimes it is
but other times it's just a reminder to sort out what you'll forget and
what you'll miss

i am far from perfect
more so an expert in being the furthest thing from it
i am not just another human being
i am the surface on which you walk and the air that keeps you
breathing

different skin

it's okay to not feel okay
if you look closely, you'll see the light in every bitter day
you don't deserve this, don't blame yourself
i'll build your heaven and destroy your hell

look into my eyes, i'm a beat and broken man
struggling to live this life the best way that i can
and i've seen the weakest of us fall
but i refuse to go down like a wrecking ball

i'm not strong, no i never even came close
i'm no stranger to hopelessness but i never let it show
i'm strangled with mistakes and i'm drowning in regrets
thinking about the end should never mean acting upon it

we all share the same heart but we all wear different skin
we all hurt inside, but only in the body that we're in
let me feel your heartache and let me feel your pain

i'd rather take the blame if saving you drives me insane

i used to pour out my guts into gold
until i hurt so many times that it all turned to stone
i will always blame myself
i just hope you're doing well

heart brakes

i've never felt so sick before

picturing his lips and body on yours
how can i let go when i all wanna do is hold on?
how can i miss you if you're never gone?
just because you're not here with me
doesn't mean i'll ever leave

this is my pain, this has become my life
running away from everything i tried to leave behind
but it keeps coming back to me, all i want is for you to come back to
me
fix this mess, fix our dreams
piece back together what we wanted to be
but now i'm miserable and alone
i hate to accept that i'm better off on my own

your whole world turns upside down
when you watch the person you love find love in someone else
maybe that's not what it seems at first
but i'd be lying if i said it didn't hurt

i'm not just heartbroken, i'm brokenhearted
the only difference is one i accept and the other you started

i can't look at you without picturing him
i can't think about you without wishing i didn't
i can't love you anymore but i still do
how am i still standing after everything you put me through?

a bullet through a flock of doves

have you ever noticed how whispers turn into echoes?
it's always the smaller things that are the hardest to let go
but even if i replay this all out in my head
there's nothing that can take away the pain from the things i've said

my only fear is the fear of myself
i regret to remember the stories i'd tell
maybe if everything was perfectly placed, i wouldn't have to run
i wouldn't have to lie just to escape a world i thought i won

i am easily broken, i am easily bent
i have trouble deciding what is exactly my intent
is it to prove to myself that i'm better than the world around me or is
it to lead my shadow into corners that only i can see?
speak my name, the blackest of words
far from a king is what i have heard

becoming a bullet through a flock of doves
is the feeling of falling to somewhere above
never asleep, i'm never awake
lost in myself while my time is at stake
becoming a hero in a place before time

only makes you a burden, not one of a kind

i of the storm

once the sky comes falling down on me
the end of the world is all i'll need
to put the eye of the storm at ease
because the "i" of the storm has always been me
so, if you want to, let me breathe
but i'll understand if you want me to leave
you don't need every piece to fill in the missing peace
just look past the rain, embrace it and repeat

to be honest...

nothing in life gets better, take it from me, it only gets worse
i would do anything to let myself free of this curse
you see, i was born with a heart and i was born with a mind
but everything i've ever wanted has always been trapped inside
i've never seen happiness and i've never traveled its path
i can't tell you the last time i've had anything good in my life last

i always tell myself i wanna be taken away from this place
but i'm too much of a coward to stare death in the face
and what makes me more of a coward is i can't even stand up to the
life i lead in front of me
why bother having dreams if i can't ever find the means to fall
asleep?
it's my very conscience and my bitter thoughts that leave me awake
at night
you would've thought i'd be stronger from putting up with this
constant fight

there's no such thing as depression, it's called life
it's called being overwhelmed, and watching your sanity pass like
the time
i never meant to hurt anyone, but in the end i've only hurt myself

to be honest, i think that pain is the only thing i've ever felt

burden

right now, i'll be honest, i'd rather not be alive
but hear me out, i really don't want to die
i just want the pain to stop
i just want the last grain of sand in the hourglass to drop
so i can flip it over, and start over again
but first let me down this bottle of ambien
and fall out of consciousness and into something beyond REM sleep
i welcome death, but now i wonder will it welcome me?
is there a lesson to be learned? or am i destined just to burn?
will i maybe reach the pearl encrusted gates? or when i arrive, will i
be too late?
is there nothing after the final curtain call? then what exactly is the
point of any of this at all?
is there a higher power or are we alone?
is this some sort of projection?
or am i one in a million simultaneously living, breathing, thinking
clones?
but aside from the big questions…
i sit here in my own small conscious mind
and wonder why i even grasp the concept to wonder why
i wonder why i'm stuck in a mind like this
why i'm constantly feeling as if the deepest enigmas of my mind are
a slowly deteriorating abyss
i wonder why i hate the person i've grown to be
i'm so sick of seeing happy people in my dreams and on the streets
i just want to be like them…
i just want to be the person that can wake up every day and feel
confident
wake up every day with some sort of sense of accomplishment
but instead i feel like a ghostly figure just getting in the way of
everyone around me

even if i stand in an empty room, i still feel as if my presence is unsettling

i hate the things i'm supposed to love

i need to forget to remember and i need the feeling of feeling numb

have you ever been so scared of yourself that you're afraid to laugh?

that you're afraid to speak?

that you're afraid to love?

have you ever lived your life with the notion that you're living just to constantly be judged?

because that's how i feel and that's how i've always felt

i can't be scared of death if i've already experienced hell

so take one step inside of my shoes and i promise you that you'll trip over the laces

i promise you that you'll feel lost in all of what seems like the most familiar places

i need you to take one look into my eye

tell me it's okay to die

tell me that the world will still keep turning even when i'm not alive

it's getting too hard for me here, i've always excelled in learning how to disappear

because when you're a burden, just like me

you dance like the wind and in an instant, i'm finally free

immortal

sometimes i need to remind myself that it's okay to die
there's blood on my hands and it helps snap me back to life
purgatory, reality, we're all just somewhere in between
just hope that you never end up like me
i slit my own throat just to see what it feels like
i'll cover the wound just to open it another time

the taste of medicine is smooth
helps me forget the bitterness of you
watch me swallow a knife and puncture my lungs
watch me as i'm gasping for air but i'm still holding on
I'm immortal, you know
i sold my soul for gold

can i have your attention?
i'm running of room for discretion
i guess the entire world will know my plan
self-deluded and destructive dominance

run away from me, run as far as you can
i'm a ticking time bomb and i forgot how long i have

i'll put a bullet in between my eyes
is the grass really greener on the other side?
what if those colors don't really exist?
then what the hell is the point in all of this?

i need you to jump
jump right off the edge with me
i need you to drown
and ask me how deep should it be

i'll lose my grip
i can only hope that you will too
we need to die

will you kill me or will i kill you?

soul eater

nobody can save you from yourself
heaven is only a reflection of hell
when you see life is perspective
and reality is perception
a dream can act an elegant ballet
is it a nightmare that's been balancing preservation and decay?

i am nature in its finest form
a ghost of what my past has worn
a heart on one sleeve and an eye on the other
beating back and forth between greys and vivid colors

i'm not the solitude that you will you seek
i'm the very moment that you will always repeat
the intention here was never to haunt your dreams
but i assume that for some reason, you don't want me to leave
i'm not the eagle, i'm the crow
i'm someone that you should never know
i won't stop you if you want to sell your soul

because i've been fine since i lost mine a long time ago

just like paper airplanes

let me start my story at the end
because that's really where all of this begins
take me back to a time when being alive felt that way
before better vibes and better days started to feel like a bittersweet
and distant place

i never fell apart, i only had a chance to crash upon my own weight
at once
it was never a process, it was just something i was forced to become
and i never meant to turn the world against me
but i can't help but to feel helpless and alone
i set my entire life on fire
and i'm stuck figuring out if i'm better off melting or living in the
cold

i didn't disappear, i just had to get away
time is only perception so i'll be back at another date
if you promise not to wait for me, i'll wrap your words in gold
because i know at some point they'd rust, just like everything else
that i was ever told

am i determined to be forgotten?
maybe i could just blend in as an unlikely option
i'm like a paper airplane skimming across a shallow lake
there isn't room to drown but there's room to meet a likely fate
when your only purpose fails you, the weakest thing can kill you
it's not about the sky and the reason why it's blue

it's the answer that you'll never find, because the question never
found you

my: self

i'm not scared of myself
is what i try to tell myself
i used to speak up for myself
until i lost sight of myself

i'm not a coward, just a man lost in the definition of that
there's a thing called confidence and i'd do anything to have it back
i had a voice and i had a heart
too many things tore them both apart

death is something that i've met before, it's even come to learn my name
and every time it knocks on my door, it takes something that i love away
so maybe i should run, would it matter if i hide?
i'm so used to failing, does it matter if i try?
i stopped asking for help, and now i only ask why
i'm too scared of my own shadow to even feel alive

i live alone in a crowded room
trapped with the thoughts of what i've been and will go through
my darkness, in secret, eats me alive
somewhere along the way, i found myself lost in the light

it's the first step onto solid ground
when everything suddenly comes crashing down
when it rains, it always finds a way to pour
i miss the life i used to have, the one that i don't have anymore

i can't be the only one here
that's drowning in all of my fears

my lungs can't handle the water
i don't want all of this to be over
i just need to get rid of the pain
the one that i bear with each day

i may not see eye to eye with the world that i live in
if you pretend to be blind, one day things will only seem more vivid
don't ever take for granted, the things you didn't know you could
take in such a way
because time has a place and an unjustified reason to take those
things away

do things only get better or do they get worse?
they say to count your blessings, but what if you've always been
cursed?
what if i pretend i'm not real?
would i still recollect everything that i feel?
i wish i could make it all go away
me, myself and i will learn to live with better days

my body is a vessel, and my mind lives out at sea
capturing the dullest dreams and releasing every useful part of me
if can't count on the waves to bring me to normality
will i ever wash ashore to relive reality?

they say pain is only weakness leaving the body, but we all know it
never leaves our hearts
it's the struggle to face the fact that things can't change, and that's
always the hardest part
so you can cover up these scars and let time heal all your wounds
it'll never change who you are or anything that you have been
through

the biggest piece of my heart

something i'll never forget and always remember
is when i got the news in late december
that you were sick and hurting
but you were strong and reassuring
you told me that you would be okay
you told me that your pain would go away

my mother, my best friend
my everything until the very end
you made me laugh, you kept me safe
you made feel okay even when i was in my darkest place
and something like this you never get over, you only learn to deal
something like this is something i never thought i'd ever feel

you stayed strong and we stayed strong with you
i remember when the doctors said that there was nothing more that
they can do
we cried together, and i remember the look in your eyes
i remember you holding me telling me that you weren't ready to die
and in that moment, i knew my life was falling apart
and in that moment, i started losing the biggest piece of my heart

cancer
it's a word no one ever wants to hear
it's worse than your worst nightmare, it's worse than your deepest
fear
cancer
it's what tears you apart
and when you imagine hell, this is where it starts
cancer
it's what turns your lips from red to blue

it's what suffering looks like when i'm without you

it was 11:30 in the morning, late july
everyone who loves you stood by your bedside
the hardest part was that you couldn't speak, and you were half
asleep
you opened your eyes when you heard my voice
i reminded you that you had a choice
but i told you it was okay to leave
because we both knew that your pain would ease

but when you watch someone die, when you watch your whole
world pass you by
your breaths start to shorten, your bones become stiff
you reflect on everything you've ever had and loved to begin with
and when your skin becomes white as a ghost
you remember who you need the most
so i held your hand as your soul left the room
and in that moment i knew that a part of me would always be with
you

make sure

it all comes down to the one person that we can spot in a crowded
room
that moment of safety when all hell breaks loose
when the world comes to an end, will you be the one holding my
hand?
i'll be the one holding my breath
diving into the ocean so you could have room to stand
on the burning bridge of life and death
i knew you were stronger than me to begin with
and even though i promised you i would never change
i had to just to make sure that you'd be safe
once a man, now a coward
i know you'll still love me in my darkest hour

this is my desperation
to become the voice of a generation
and i can only hope that the heights we aim to reach
become more than just the phrases that we preach

#survivors

we are all survivors

there is something in all of us
embedded in our past, buried with debris and dust
wipe the surface clean
underneath we all started with a dream
somehow somewhere along the way
we lost ourselves with promises we made

we all have a story to tell
some with words, others with whistles and bells
it's a matter of reason, it's all in the tone of voice
so believe me when i say the moves that i made are all a concept of choice

starting from nothing, we can't all start from the top
and with the world in front of me, i can't and i won't stop
chasing what i believe, chasing what will become of me
even if i fall over my steps, to live for what i love is well worth the debt

we all are hurt, we all are broken, we all are weak
we all are force-fed the definition of defeat
a broken heart and a dying soul, is something that i don't see growing old
but the skin that i wear and this mind that i weave
it grows inside me and tells me i'm too strong to leave

we are all survivors—of what this life has handed us
we are all survivors—of struggle, love and lust
we are all survivors—beaten down with words of hate

we are all survivors—i am a result of fate

what is hope? what is faith?
where am i? what is my name?
am i lost or is this is my life?
i can't tell if i'm insane or just ready to die
something in me tells me i will be okay,
something is struggling with a choice to stay
i'm not confused, i'm just torn
i'm not under the weather, but i am the storm
i'm not okay, and i'm not fine
surviving this, surviving time

survivors
raise your hands, raise your voice
survivors
i am reborn, i am the leader of rejoice
survivors
wear it on your skin, wear your heart on your sleeve
we all are kings and queens, as long as you believe

survive yourself, revive your mind
and learn to live again
the surreal survival of inevitable denial

you will learn to live again

the spirit system

are we dreaming or just alive?
can the difference be justified?
because i've found the fraud that links the concept of time
to the meaningful meaningless point of our lives

it's like a shape shifting atmosphere
colliding our hopes with things that only seem to appear
can you notice all the subtle hints life throws at you?
or maybe you're not real, it guess it depends on the users point of
view

listen to me, listen to every word i have to say
because we are the purest form of souls…
we are everything that the system needs to stay awake
our bodies are a vessel to a greater, larger unknown
heavens a lie when you look through a microscope
the things that keep us awake at night
the things that make us question what is and isn't right
is far from our reach, yet it's somehow ours to keep
but that's the beauty of it all, to create something just to watch it fall

isn't that the dream?
to gain the knowledge of what it means to be?
we're so much more than obedient sheep
we're a product of space and the space in between
if you can't find the answers, at least ask the question
will you live your life graciously or leave as an unopened message?

there's a difference between living and being alive
every breath you've ever taken has been in a different rhythm of time
just so you can see, life isn't all what it seems

even the simplest of things can hold so much more meaning

and it all comes down to this
when you break it down, even your god is a myth
a mind controlled makes for the greatest story ever told
take the science as truth, even the wisest of men are born to lose

theories of big bangs don't make any sense
because every nothing needs something even if it is nothing to begin
with
there's more that the naked eye will never see
you're more than you and i'm more than me
we're not ghosts, we're just drifters lost at sea
traveling through one life to see what the next one brings
a lucid dream, one that jolts you from your sleep
so maybe that's life, and when we die, everything repeats

i feel like i'm gone with the wind
thinking back to when i was a kid
time stood still just like the sound of space
blind to the thought of any type of change

monsters

they used to tell me that monsters are hiding under my bed
but now that i've grown, i've learned that they actually exist inside of
my head
my thoughts are my nightmares and my dreams are my fears
i'm scared of every little thing that could leave my conscience clear

a clouded mind for troubled times
become the martyr you left behind
in disbelief, in sincerity
kind-heartedness was never a friend to me
with desperate times come desperate measures
a traveler through the worst of weather
we are the storm and the calm before it hits
learn the difference between fire, flames and the spark that we lit

everything we know is either said or has been done
the heart that changed me, now blacker than the sun
the end of times or the worst of times?
i'll never know which one is mine
so let me stumble and let me fall
i knew you wouldn't be there in the end after all

this is my first attempt at a second chance
holding my breath like i'm holding this branch
so scared to let go and to just be myself
how can i not face something i know all too well?

maybe i was the monster all along
i knew i could never learn what's right from what's wrong
if i can't teach myself to break down my walls
why should i bother even living at all?

setting fire

i can't stop feeling like my shadow is nothing but a ghost
following me constantly and haunting me with the things i miss the
most
i can't control the things that i think, only the things that i say
the only difference is, is that i wish that all of those things would go
away
i wanna feel numb, somewhere far from alive
somewhere between being buried up to my neck and trying not to
die
the pressure becomes harder and the surface begins to crack
i thought i was doing better…
but my dreams have faded from vivid colors to the darkest shade of
black

watch me let the floor cave in beneath me
when i start to care again, it'll lose all of its meaning
there's more to this, or so it seems
i can pretend that i'm okay, i can pretend to be at peace
i can pretend to be at ease, i can pretend to chase a dream
let's face the fact that i'm paralyzed and my heart can't keep track of
its beats

i can't imagine the thought of suffocating but living with the
consistent thought of wonder is equally worse
there's something inside of me far much worse than pain…
it's the very thing that defines the word "hurt"
i can reminisce, but the memories always find a way to let
themselves go
maybe that's my mind's way of telling me i'm too far gone to hold a
place of its own

set fire to everything that keeps me awake at night
i'd rather choke on the ashes if it'll help things seem alright
i'll climb to the highest realm just to try to see my past again

even if i fall to my death, i'll finally have a place to fit in

i just disappeared

sometimes the entrapment of loneliness keeps growing on me
it has me in a chokehold and is refusing to let me breathe
the last thing i want to do is suffocate on the thing i hate the most
but if it consumes me while i'm alive, will it still consume me as a
ghost?

it's like my sadness is the seed that planted everything i've ever
feared
the roots are spreading farther, that much i know is clear
what if i grow into a poisonous plant that even i'm too afraid to
touch?
let the earth become one with my soul, but i'm sure even that won't
be enough

i never wanted to be buried alive but the passing of time has already
done that on its own
i don't even know who dug my grave or who left me destined to be
alone

i lost sight of what love is, and i'm too afraid to gain it back so i'll rip
out my eyes
i'll lead my life blind and leave the sensation of attraction behind
i'm so sick of wearing my heart on my sleeve so i'll chop off all my
limbs
this way it'll be easier to resist your schemes and fall into your tricks
and when the worst is over, i know that i'll still care
please tie me to the tracks so i can spill my guts from here to there

maybe i'm meant to be on my own
or maybe i wasn't meant to be anything at all
was i some sort of mistake?

i feel like i shouldn't be here in the first place
am i karma? maybe i'm just the bad side of it
because everything i do always has a consequence
i'm sorry for the burden that i always knew i'd be
maybe if i'm gone, it'll bring light to your long lost peace
i know i'm nothing special, so i'll go away, i know that you don't
need me here
you can find me somewhere in the distance, because today is the day
that i just disappeared

sun(blind)

i wish i saw the sun as blinding
but then i turn around and instead, i let it guide me
i'll keep walking and walking until the seasons start to change
things will work out if you just let them turn the page
life is a story, and your actions, they write it
reality is only a matter of perspective
so i'll change course, and i'll walk towards the sun
sometimes it hurts my eyes when i stare for too long
but life without pain is only life without learning right from wrong

i used to look forward to the rain
i used to find comfort in reminiscing about all of my pain
but then i came to realize, there's more to life, there are better days
if i can't change time, i should learn to change my ways

i'll never let my nightmares change my mind
and i'll never let my dreams be the things that i leave behind
i'll take my heart, i'll rip it out, and i'll hold it to the sky

and i'll let the sunshine be the one to change my life

everything to me

the more days that go by, the harder it is to face reality
it's as if i'm in denial of everything that's been put in front of me
will you ever be okay again?
will things go back to how they were back then?
i know it's hard for you to be yourself
but just know i'm one with your pain and i'm living in hell

sometimes saying i love you just isn't enough
there's something more than this, i'm begging you to never give up
you're the one that raised me and you made me who i am
i hope that i've made you proud because i've done the best i can

i feel so close to you, but at the same time, i feel like i'm miles away
because i can't answer the question when i ask myself if things are
okay
all i want is to make all of your dreams come true
i need you to be strong so i can live out all your dreams with you

i'd be lying if i said that you meant everything to me
you mean more than that, more than the world will ever see
let me shine a light on every promise that i've made to you
we can watch it all burn bright as i give you all i've ever wanted

i wish it was my heart that's broken, but instead it's my life
all i wish is for the time to come when i don't cry myself to sleep
every night
i will teach myself to be strong, but only for you
and i know you'll be okay again, just keep holding on and keep
pushing through

take it from me
don't ever mistake a misconception for a missed conception
sometimes you need to analyze the things you'll grow to realize
because if you see past the passing of time
has it even passed at all?

somewhere in the distance

i fell in love once and it was the best and the worst thing that's ever
happened to me
you see, i always thought having someone was something that i
need
but now that i've lost it, i've realized i was right, it's like cutting off
my air to breathe
i can't depend on myself, i'm too weak for that
i don't care enough to change, i know how to keep my anxious mind
in tact

i miss the feeling of feeling something new
i miss wondering if things are happening too soon
i miss a certain you, the one i couldn't help but grow into
and it kills me to know that you're with someone new
i won't move on, but i'll get through

listen to me closely, you may not think there's a difference
whether you're with me or somewhere in the distance
but i'm addicted to who you are and the life you live
i can't run away if i'm struggling to begin with
i regret not being better, i regret not doing so much more
and now i've lost my future, i've lost the reason that i live for

light me a candle and blow it out so i can symbolize what i lost and
what i can't gain back
i'm the burnt out flame that now turned into melted wax
i'm the god you grew to realize was only a myth
when you uncover that i wasn't really so great to begin with
but, i'll always promise you the world and you will always have my
heart
that's something that has never changed from the very start

i hope that you're happy, i just wish you were happy with me
i hate that he's everything that i failed to be
friends until the end is all i'll ever ask
and in this moment, you were my first true love, and you were my
very last

if i could hold you one more time, maybe just for forever and a day
i could live with peace just knowing that with you i'll be okay

devil

i wish i knew how to keep my dreams alive
the only thing i know anymore is how to leave what matters most
behind
how can i stand up to a bright future when i keep tripping over a
dark past?
how can i be expected to keep track of time if nothing at all ever
lasts?

i held hands with the devil and his palms felt a lot like mine
little did i know…
i've been losing a battle with all of the demons i suppressed in the
back of my mind
if you ever wondered what it was just like to feel just like me

take a look at yourself and hate everything about the person you see

time bomb

i keep on losing everything that matters to me
and everything that matters to me is everything that makes me feel
like me
how am i supposed to get up, get out and move on without your help
how am i supposed to see past everything that's made my life a
living hell

if a negative mind is self-destructive
consider me a ticking time bomb
i'm trapped in something that i can never get out of
i never wanted to be this way, so thank you for making me this way
if in the end, i lose my life, you're the only one there is to blame

I'mperfection

i never said i was afraid to die
to be honest i'm more scared of being alive
i'd rather lose love than let love lose me
i'm well-adjusted to the lies that i'm fed rather than the truth that i
seek

the first time i started to get a real taste for the world, i started
choking on my tongue
it's the times i needed to feel alive when my body feels completely
numb
if you've ever felt like me, like you're constantly alone in a crowded
room
hold onto the concept of hope because that's the one thing you can
never lose

i never said i was perfect, or that any of us ever would be
but there's more than just the damage that you allow the world to see
i'm terrified of my own shadow
because my past is the only thing that i would let follow me
it's what helps me grow to break these chains that'll be able to set me
free

i have learned one thing...
i am not made of imperfections
i'm made from "i'm perfection"

we all have reflections, but none of us view them the same
there's always a finger to point but sometimes get lost in finding the
blame

hold each other's fear of letting go

and let go of the fear of holding on
we are not made of imperfections
we are made from "i'm perfection"

seasons, as they speak

there's no better time than now
to pick up every piece that's fallen down
i'm not the avalanche that came and went
i'm the winter that you wished would always end

listen to the seasons, i am the voice of justified reason
and just like the spring, i'll blossom and i'll fade
into the summer where we can shine and swim our dreams away

dream of autumn, dream of fall
the most beautiful dance among them all
watch the leaves change, watch them blow away
we always wish things could stay this way
life is like the seasons and people come and go
it's not about who or what sticks around, all that matters is that you
grow
life is like the seasons and people come and go
the things you own you'll soon forget but you'll never lose the things
you know

too close for comfort

i distance myself from everyone
but not because of the things i've done
but because the things i might do
just remember that i'd hurt myself before i ever hurt you
pain changes the way a person thinks and the way a person sleeps
it makes you scared to be alone even in your dreams
i walk down an unmarked road, just to find out where it goes
even if i'm paralyzed, that'll never stop my searching soul
from moving on to something better
moving on to something strong
even in the worst of weather
an eternity may not seem so long
i'd prefer rain because i feel at home when i'm in a storm
the thunder helps me sleep and the darkness keeps me warm
sometimes i like to know what it's like to miss the sun
you lose sight of the light when you're face to face with the barrel of
a gun
i never knew how much too much really was
but now it's clear what so much torment has done
i need to be forgotten, i need to let go and to be let go
don't hold onto something that you will never know
was i ever really here, or was i just a ghost?

more scared to live than i was to die, reality is a comfort that has
come far too close

the only thing holding me back is being held back
i can't be expected to follow my heart if my footsteps can't keep pace
of their own tracks

---

i had a panic attack thinking about you
i guess i'll always question what i ever did to you
moving on is always the first move
but the hardest is accepting that i'll have to

---

let's turn it back a notch to a much simpler time
i could take on the world, now i'm scared to be alive
i know i hurt you, i must live with that
you know i hurt too, have you ever thought of that?
i let the worst of me take over the best in me
...and i lost everything

disappear

i took my soul out from my body and left it somewhere far away
somewhere along the lines, my mind wandered off
and now i'm either dreaming or learning how to use my brain
it's so fucked up, you see
how a single moment could either leave you in total ecstasy
or define the thing we all consider to be misery

i'm not crazy, i know that much
but i'm not sane, it's just that things are rough
so i stay stable here
in the little gray room, or so it appears
through all the mist, it all becomes crystal clear
this is my one chance to disappear

things can't get worse if they never get better
suck it up because life changes like the weather
i'm nothing to cry about, just another lost soul incomplete and filled
with doubt
no, i'm not sorry
if that's what you're wondering

i had a dream last week
i almost died in it, so i woke up, laughed and fell back asleep
one can wish, i said
oh, the thought of being dead
listen to me ramble about the crazy thoughts that run through my
head

is it fucked up of me to think those things?
because it's kind of hard when i know that i'm the worst part of me
is it my fear to live? or is it that i live in fear?
if you pretend that i was never here
it's as if i never disappeared

self-victim

if i shook hands with reality
it'd have the hardest grip, but eventually let go
if i lost my mind, but found my heart
the blood in my veins would pump a life i've never known

i'm losing touch, i'm becoming numb
i'm blind and deaf, finding comfort in coming undone
my roots are unraveling, i'm cast to stone, leaving the past behind
the strength i found within myself
is something I've been longing to find

all my life i've seen myself as insignificant
but everything that has brought me to this point has shown me that
i'm in significance

my dreams don't act as idols
it's every mistake i have made that showed me the ropes
and the harder i pull, the closer i am to becoming the man i was born
to be

never trust the calm before the storm
because when all is said and done
you're left in ruins, and sleeping in debris

i never claimed to be a victim
i came here at my own will

i've learned my lessons, i've paid my dues
it seems like breathing underwater is something that i've become
used to
there's still a surface ready for me to reach
it's only a matter of time before i can feel free

it's the struggle and it's all of my fears
that'll make me stronger than these tears

you can run from your past and chase the life you want to lead
just like the wind chases the leaves that fall from a growing tree

if i can find hope in black holes

just know it's not worth it to let go

observer

sometimes i wonder what would happen if i lost touch with the
world and my body began to float
would i miss the sudden change of seasons or the earth beneath my
toes?
if gravity is the only thing keeping me level-headed, then take it
away and show me the way to heaven
because sometimes i feel like being alive seems more a crime
when you see the world from my open eyes after observing the
passing of time

my god hasn't abandoned me, i've just come to grips with how
reality was meant to be seen
to live free from a myth, and live from within
to become your own man, to fall again and again until you learn to
stand

broken mirrors

i once was the architect of an empire
but i let it fall and i let it sink beneath the ground
it's like when you have a light but possess the fear to let it shine
sometimes what really matters isn't important
it's only the thought behind it that stands for something

like statues, we are all bound to fall
but give praise to the ones who held us up
and just like the sky, we all have something to reach for
but we'd rather use our eyes to find the answers

we are but blind mice asking questions of our surroundings
how does anything give meaning? when will the details come to
life?
maybe the world is just a living dream hiding under a grand disguise

build me and tear me down
you'll never see the same side of me again
i am a monster built of debris
chasing my tail and trying to piece myself back together

forever doesn't seem like a long time when you're unconscious for
most of it
share your memories with me
so i don't have to live in a world where someone like me exists

i am the parallel, a breathing house of mirrors
just because one side is more clear than the other doesn't mean that
it's not there
i've looked over my shoulder only to find a perching crow
am i the better of two evils?

or maybe we're both the same…

disconnected from reality
i have created time
leave me with my new discoveries

a beating heart and a racing mind

cycles

it seems crazy that we're only told that there's light in the darkness
well i've seen darkness in the light
and it's all too real, and all too much to handle

life is nothing but a vicious cycle that will only eat you alive and spit
you back out
and as you try piecing yourself back together
you wonder what parts you should leave exposed and which you
should cover the most
because some places have seen more damage than others

and i'll admit, there are days when i miss everything about you
but most of the time, i leave my past in the past and don't bother
looking back
it's just hard when the things that used to remind me of you
start holding meaning to me again

maybe because you were the only one that understood me
maybe because you were the only one that could put up with the real
me

i've accepted that things will never the same again
but that doesn't mean that i don't wish for things to change

i never was the one to cast a stone, but once i did, it was the only one
to sink

i can't feel the weight of the world
if i'm paralyzed and numb
and i can't just let things stay this way
when we know that we're both too stubborn to make things change

so, before i self-destruct, let me leave you with one last thought
i was never your shoulder to cry on, i was just a walking apology
in the end we all pretend the pain isn't real
in the end we are all like mannequins
standing still in a world that keeps moving
we turn our heads but we still see the same things

why raise your voice if you can raise your heart?

i'd rather hold high something i've had from the start

live your legacy

we are nothing more than words that flow from the mind
and we are put here by the ink of predetermined space and time
but i'd like to think that there is life in death
so when i leave, i'll become something more than just a body at rest

i am the earth, the wind, and the sea
and there is much more on the inside than what you make of me
you see, i've been through heaven and i've seen hell
will we ever know the truth? i guess that only time will tell

tell me everything i want to hear
i am a god, strong enough to face my fears

there is so much more after the light in the dark
these are the tracks you leave, and where you choose to make your
mark
i've traveled too far to let this journey go to waste
sailing along the shore, i found what i needed to restore my faith

on this compass, it never read which way to go
in every corner, each letter spells out 'hope'
because i know i can make this world my home
if i search within myself, my heart will tell me where i'm meant to
go

i have found the meaning of time
it is to create out of it what is rightfully mine

this is my legacy
i'll leave you with these memories
this is my heart and soul
my dreams won't die so easily

the greatest fraud

i could never see myself as a catalyst for a tireless war
all i ask is to live for something that i can be proud of standing for
my unraveling roots travel the untraveled road
with every move that i make, another branch begins to grow

they say you can count wisdom by the pattern of falling leaves
picture a tree with growing branches
each and every one all standing for a dream
and with every leaf that falls
another life is touched and changed
just because you can't alter minds, doesn't mean you can't change it's
place

we all stand differently on what will be a similarity
and in the end, inevitably we will all fall to singularity

dividing minds only leads to subtracting lives
i am a metaphor for war
i am what you thought you stood for

don't fall short to the changing of times
a rapid pace of heart will soon uncover the crimes
shame has swallowed you whole, spit you out, and left you for dead
if your shadow is as dark as your secrets, don't dare call yourself
heaven sent

this isn't a way of life, it never has and never will be

there's something greater than myself, it's not a god, it's another part
of me

body bags at formal events

there's a black cloud constantly hanging over my head
dragging me closer to every beginning's end
without a second chance, and not even a first
every scar that i've ever had just appeared and wasn't given the time
to hurt
i'm a walking wound, the emotionally deserted
a living mess, struggling to learn what i did to deserve this

i want to leave my mark, a special place inside your heart
just like leaving footprints in wet concrete
or living out one another's dreams
but we all get hurt somehow in the end
love seems to make as much sense

as body bags at formal events

conclusions

i am the seeker of truth
and what will set me free
the only thing that's been hiding
is the very thing that's composing me
lies to hide what is real
and a soul built on nothing but the intent to steal
what is golden, what is pure
build me from greed and i'll keep begging for more

you can't ignore the sky if you're granted the gift to see
you can't fall out of reach if your hands are the ones that choose to feed
how can you pretend to comprehend what's intended
when what lies ahead has fallen behind, became the median, a severing knot from a truth that's been tied

i don't need hope, i only need you
help me find the strength to push through what i'm going through
fragile and hanging from my seams
i'd rather lose my mind than lose all of my dreams

i can't jump to conclusions standing in the shallow end

i'll take my time to let this unfold so i can pull apart truth from pretend

i hope that you have wings in heaven
but for now, i'll just keep second guessing
i hope i made you happy, and i hope that you were proud of me
you've always been the spitting image of the person that i want to be
i may seem happy here, but to tell the truth, i'm lost
i need you more than anything

beyond forever

this is where my story begins
the day i found out you were sick
we told each other everything would be okay
eight months later and nothing was the same

a piece of me died with you in that room
sometimes i refuse to believe what i've been through
like this was all a bad dream
hoping i would wake up with some sort of peace
but time doesn't heal, you just learn to deal with it
sometimes the cards that you end up with are not the ones you
started with

my entire world shifted upside down that day
six years later and i still don't feel okay

will i ever feel okay?
will the pain ever go away?
it'll fade in time, but it'll still be there
it'll still leave a mark and that's still more than i could bear

i remember growing up, and i'll remember growing old
i just wish i had you here the whole time so i could have your hand
to hold
you always knew just what to say and you taught me right from
wrong
you were the greatest friend i'll ever have and i promise that i'll stay
strong

i will never find comfort in anyone other
than the beautiful soul that was my mother

you left this world way too soon
i hope you know that i'm always dreaming of you

and when i'm at my worst, show me a sign and show me that you're there
give me a reason to not feel alone and scared
i miss you more than i could ever put into words
i love you and living without you is the most i've ever hurt

losing you was a nightmare come to life
we all lost a friend, a mother, and my father lost his wife
i remember the last time you looked at me—
it was the last time you opened your eyes
i told you it was okay to go and that i would be alright
but when your heart stopped beating, i lost my mind and collapsed to the floor
i just didn't want this to be real anymore
please come back to me, i need you more than ever
i love you mom, always and beyond forever

learning to breathe underwater

every life endures pain
it's as if it's as inevitable as death itself
the key is to overcome the sensation
unlocking a door to a realm of endless sincerity and a sense of vivid
dreaming

one day you'll learn that the world was never out to crush you
the pressure will only make you stronger

it's the burdens that make you whole
and the steps you never took that bring you one step back

i've learned what it's like to sleep with both eyes open
and i've found comfort in breathing underwater

i am my own hope
standing on my own two feet
and i refuse to fall to the depths of regret

stranded on my knees

Learning To Breathe Underwater

Written By
Jason Elliot

Cover Art By
Ron Totman

Edited By
Annie O'Sullivan

Executive Editors
Bryan J Mangam
Annie O'Sullivan